LITTLE CRITTER®

ABCs

LITTLE CRITTER®
ABCs

BY MERCER MAYER

SCHOLASTIC INC.

A
airplane

bicycle

D
dog

E

eggs

F
frogs

G

guitars

H

hula hoops

I

ice-skate

J
jump

K
king

L

leaves

M

mouse

N

nest

O
owl

P

pillows

Q

quilts

R
rain

S

sun

T
toothpaste

U
underwear

V violin

W wagon

X "marks the spot"

Y yarn

Z zebra

ISBN 978-0-545-84922-7

12 11 10 9 8 7 6 5 4 3 2 1   15 16 17 18 19 20/0

Printed in the U.S.A.   40

First Scholastic printing, January 2015

A Big Tuna New Media LLC/ J.R. Sansevere Book